MY EPISODES WITH SANVI

A MOM TO MOM CONNE[...]

GOWTHAMI MOHAN

I dedicate this book to my Mom and to my late father, who are always an inspiration to me to start new things without any hesitation. I always feel that their blessings are showered on us.

Contents

Contents

Preface

This is a book of lessons "By a mother To all mothers". I strongly believe that all the lessons I learnt with my daughter should be shared with other mothers. It is A mom to mom connect material where you can feel the naughtiness of your child, beautiful moments of your life, the essence and achievements of your motherhood through us. I assure you that you will see yourself and your little one while reading this book. Step into the world where you felt yourself as a complete human. Happy reading.

Acknowledgements

This is my time to pay honor to my beloved husband Mohan, who is always there as my backbone in everything I do. He is a person, next to my mom, who doesn't restrict me anytime to do whatever I feel. He lets me explore the world and is supportive of all my decisions. Sometimes we get stuck or our decisions may go wrong but even in those hard times, he will not blame me for such a situation, instead he helps me come out of the situation by extending his maximum support. In simple words, I can say, I am lucky to have him as my husband and Sanvi as my daughter. These two humans made my life colorful and meaningful.

Gratitude

My special thanks to my two beautiful friends Ms. Pramila Shamraj and Ms. Ritika Sen , who has edited my book in spite of their busy schedules. Ms.Ritika Sen is the sole reason for motivating me to start the book. Also I extend my thanks to my family members, who supported me in this process of publishing the book. As we think,we are. It's my honor to thank the universe, where I had sowed my thoughts, which in turn made my thoughts into a book on a planned day.

CHAPTER ONE

A Warm Welcome

As the years pass by, we learn many things from the surroundings and the people we come across.Sometimes, we feel special when we are honoured by our little ones' actions, when they do something for us, unexpectedly. In the course of our busy schedule, it will drive our mood to different tracks. In fact, that feeling will instantly restore our positivity.

My little girl is in lower kindergarten, her school gets over by afternoon 1 o' clock. I am a working woman who will come back home by evening 5 o' clock. I have to climb 4 floors, as our apartment doesn't have a lift.The moment she sees me parking my vehicle from the Balcony of our house, she will come down to the 3rd floor to pick up my lunch bag or atleast the water bottle with the warm welcome smile on her face.She will continue the gesture with the questions like, why haven't you drunk enough water today? Did you eat your snacks or lunch? Etc.,

These things from my little girl will not only bring happiness to me but also the revival to play and spend extra time with her that day. If I express my gratitude towards her actions, she will repeat that beautifully in the upcoming days too.

As a mom, it will be a delight to receive such a welcome, that gives me a refreshing evening to do my work with the same energy that I had during the day time. Sometimes my complaints at my workplace or mood that I carry forward will vanish like someone swishing the magic wand. Ya Of course, My little girl is an angel, who swishes my mood with her smile.

I encourage her gesture,as her hospitality will be horned in the course of the time.This doesn't only speak about the hospitality but also the important life skill value called empathy,thinking or deciding from the others' shoes.

Some may feel that my daughter has such inbuilt quality, which should not be expected with other children, after reading this. To be honest, she has copied the skill from us. A Year before when she was in play school, we used to do the same to her, as I was at home during that time.It might have given some sort of happiness to her, that feel induces her to do the same to me this year.This is the perfect example, where a parent should understand the values can be incorporated through reciprocation.Inculcate the values or gestures to the children through your actions.

CHAPTER TWO

A Sweet Concern

It was a day, which was hectic and jam-packed.I had reached home by 8 o' clock that day. As usual my little girl received me with her warm smile.I could understand her curiosity to play with me. But I was literally tired, as I was practicing to host the ceremony the next day. So much of rehearsals and the other works signaled my brain to sleep.Immediately after my dinner , I apologized to my little world and I went to bed. The moment I lay on the bed, I lost my consciousness.

I hoped it was about half an hour of deep sleep, someone is lifting my leg. My consciousness awakened me and the scene I saw was a delight. Ya you guessed it right. My little girl placed a pillow under my legs as she could not hold my legs for a long time. For that purpose she had lifted my leg. She wasn't aware that I was awakened. She massaged my heels and legs with her little fingers. I was in tears with her unconditional love.The moment she saw that I was seeing her, she told me to take rest. As she noticed that I had very little for dinner, She brought a glass of milk to my bed and washed the glass by herself.

I was feeling happy yet tired to help her in actions.She returned to bed and started massaging my legs again.On looking into my eyes, with her innocent face and talk , she told me, why are you hurting yourself mommy, if you were not able to do the work, leave the job and be happy with me.

I got bursted into tears.I hugged her tightly. She couldn't understand what state I was in yet, she too shared her warmth.Though My heart filled with the utmost happiness, I had decided a thing firmly that day. This was not the right inference which she can obtain from me.In future she should not think that, if she could not manage anything, she can leave that easily.

She should develop a habit of hard work, perseverance and consistency in doing things. She should learn how to overcome struggles and balance life beautifully by seeing me. She should consider me as a role model for the above mentioned things.I took a vow to be a super mom on that day and had started balancing my life gracefully.

CHAPTER THREE

Pancakes in Our Kitchen

One day, My little girl asked shall we make pancakes? As I didn't have much work that afternoon,I nodded to make pancakes. I started watching videos for perfect pancakes and listed out the ingredients to prepare. Then we were set to make the pancake batter. The moment I uttered 2 cups of maida, to my wonder she asked, ``Do you measure using this measuring cup? I said yeah. But i was little hesitant that she may spill the flour.She is too determined to do that all alone only with my guidance towards measures as she told , she had also watched few videos about how to do a pancake,That leaves me puzzled now, as we both are doing the pan cakes for the first time, i am little resistant to her desire for doing alone.

Then I allowed her with one condition that, only if she put the flour into the mixing bowl without any mess, she would be allowed to prepare pancakes on her own further. She rejoiced and took the flour carefully and with my guidance she measured 2 cups and put that into a mixing bowl without any spill.This gives confidence to both to proceed further. The final ingredient is egg, though she promised she can break an egg on her own, I don't have trust in her, as if she messes it while breaking, all the other ingredients may get wasted. I had explained the same to her.

Then she asked me to wait for while, she took another bowl, broke the eggs in that(it went little messy), and stirred it with fork and with the help of strainer she poured back the eggs into the bowl.The process went on till we tasted our delicious pan cakes.I had started realizing my mistakes and analyzed where i have went wrong.

Every parent is the child's first guru.We don't know whether the kids understand this, but we have a strong feel towards that statement. Whenever a kid asks for help from us to do something, we just imagine that we have to help them to do that from the scrap, even if we are not ready to put forward a question, what is this? What do you know about this? How have you planned to do it in your own way? Do you have any idea how to finish off this?

Even if we pretend to ask such questions, we are not so patient to hear their answers. We interrupt in the middle and we declare that they are on the wrong path and we will start guiding them, how we know to do that and consider that as the so-called right way to do that.

This generation of kids needs guidance not a guru nor an assistance. Let them explore and learn.

CHAPTER FOUR

Dance with Fever

There are usually two contrary statements when one is not well: "I am not well, Just don't disturb me or I need enough sleep. I need someone to take care of me. I need some warmth." All these things are the patent from an adult or a child if they are not well. Of course I will feel weaker, when I am not well. I need care from my loved ones. With the passing years, I realize that everyone has their own health issues. Let us face our own issues lest we require another person to resolve the problem.

In the same way, I will take care of my little one, whenever she is not in a good shape.Though her dad will be paying more attention to her health, I will not compromise my part too. During one of the monsoon seasons, she was down with fever ranging 102°F.It lasted for more than three days. Unfortunately at the same time, I too got some health issues, which I felt need not be addressed and was tackling by myself.

The real problem arises when I want to balance things like taking care of my little one, household chores and of course my health.When I was off to bed, literally I could not even think what is in store for me the next day. When the situation didn't get better, for more than a week, I was totally blank. I didn't have the mindset to pay heed to anyone's instructions, both in my workplace and at home.

In that week, again my little one's fever rose to 102°F, I was worried about her health, poor intake of food. But to my surprise, she asked me to put on music and danced for a while and then she lied down.She was smiling and told "I am okay amma, You don't worry.Shall we dance together for another song?" I agreed. We danced for a while and enjoyed the evening. For that moment, I forgot about her high fever. In Fact I was reminded about it, while giving the medicine to her.

As I was about to doze off, I just realized children are angels. They have magical power to turn any kind of situation into a wonderful time.We are the one who restrict them and ourselves for the transformation. All they need is warmth and time. They have the capacity to heal themselves. I was healed along with my daughter that night.

• 8 •

CHAPTER FIVE

A Complaint from School

I was very tired that evening. I planned to sleep an hour after returning from work.As I had reached my home, My little girl received me but this time without any smile on her face. I could feel some anger. Sadness and embarrassment in her face, but I was not in the mood to inquire with her immediately. Refreshing myself I went to bed.I was about to sleep, by that time i heard a low tone of my girl. Amma you know what happened today? I expected this.Since i felt tired i thought to ask that later. These tiny people need our attention as soon as they see the person they need.Though I was not in a state to hear her thing, I don't want to neglect her feelings too.

I asked, yes darling, why my little girl is not looking good.

L.g: My teacher asked me to sit with the play school students.

Me: for what?

L.g: I didn't do anything, one of my class boys fighting with me.

Me: That might be the reason dear.

L.g: If so she should have sent the guy who created the mess right?

Me: Yeah. but may i know your part in the fight.

L.g: I swear I didn't do anything. Making me sit with my juniors embarrassed me.

Me: I wondered how mature her talk is. Okay forget about that. Now you can go to play

L.g: no i need you to talk with my teacher and demand the explanation for her actions

Me: I was shocked on seeing her determination in the words.

I don't want to avoid that, at the same time this is not such a big issue where a parent should help a child.

An idea flashed in my mind.In Front of my little girl , I called her teacher and inquired with her about the situation , also requested the teacher not to neglect their feelings. Now I turned on the phone speaker. I explained to my girl that your teacher is on line, you demand the reason to her on your own.

My little girl was a little bit hesitant, then I told it is your problem, you have to deal with it. She is quite afraid to deal with that directly. Then I demanded an explanation. Her teacher told that because of her class teacher's absence , to manage the kids, they have sent a few students to the lower class teachers.Then I thanked her and moved to my girl. Now I can feel some satisfaction on her face.

Though my plan had not worked well that day as I felt she should demand an explanation from her teacher, she understood that she has to deal with her problems.From then I had not received any complaints from her. Rather she will share her memories or experience in her class.

This is where they start learning to deal with their problems, in turn it increases both problem solving and decision making skills.

CHAPTER SIX

O Time! Please Wait

One fine Sunday, we were planning to take our little girl to a park. We had decided that after finishing our household work and pending office work, we could take her to the play area.We promised the same to her. She was helping with my household chores, so that I could finish it off soon. Then she had her lunch and slept off for a while. I had utilized that time to complete my pending office work. Unfortunately I was caught up with the work. The time galloped was more than I expected. I don't like to leave any work half done. At the same time, my husband too went out with his friend for some important work.

I was struggling to complete my office work before she woke up. It added to the pressure rather than the completion of the work.The play area would be closed in another two hours. My girl had also woken up and she started questioning me for not getting ready. I tried to explain it to her but it went in vain. Then I told her strictly that I could not take her that day. She started to argue and cry as her plan collapsed.

One side was the office pressure, which demanded the work to be completed by Sunday. On the other side, my girl was throwing tantrums on all the things coming her way. I was in complete frustration. At one point, I started suppressing the poor kid with my words and gestures.

She was crying and not ready to listen or obey. Though I was aware that it was all because of us, That day I was not in a proper state of mind to handle things. It ended up in a mess. My little girl didn't want to listen to me, as she felt that I was a promise breaker.

After a while, I had to shut down all of my work. I understood that , by that time it was too late to take her to the park. Also to bring back the harmony in the house. I was very quiet for a few minutes. Then I went to my little girl and explained my situation, which I felt she was too young to understand. She threw back her thoughts with her question; why were you doing your office work here? I need your time. I could understand that, But nothing could be changed in a day as in films or advertisements.

I don't want to make any false promises, as I knew it would take time to regularize all the things. I apologized to her for not keeping up my words. That consoled her somewhat. I had decided to finish off my work at the office and to talk with the authorities about the importance of work-life balance. Sometimes the authorities in the office also behave like children, though they understand the situation, they need their work to be done on time. Then I decided finally to maintain harmony in both the places.

As we are the only saviours for our situations.

CHAPTER SEVEN

My Little Sculptor

If someone is constantly supporting you and protecting you from everyone, without judging you or your point of views? How would you feel? Apart from arguments, having someone's back without being judgemental, we will develop enormous strength. It does wonders to an individual.

My little girl backs me up without any judgement. She will always be there to protect me. Right from banter with my husband to serious arguments with anyone inside or outside my family, she would simply say " Whatever it is, My mom is correct. Don't argue with her." She would push me inside the nearby room and say, "Amma, what shall I do? Do you want water? Shall I massage your head? Come, I will help you sleep?". She will defend me from everyone, everywhere.The way she pacifies me and protects me is just beyond words.

You may argue that "supporting someone blindly will cloud their judgments. You should teach your child to analyse both sides and ask them to make the right decision." But for those who put forth these arguments, we all need unconditional love and support in our lives, instead of judgemental and prejudiced individuals.

Though I need the same, I don't want my girl to support me blindly, I have started rectifying my mistakes after seeing her defence. I try to sculpt myself into a wonderful human to make her beliefs justifiable. In course of time, I have stopped arguing for unnecessary reasons. Even in arguments, I try to put forth only the valid points. I have stopped blaming anyone in front of my child. Also I have started avoiding throwing tantrums of any kind.

Although I have started working on myself, my daughter's beliefs sculpts me into a masterpiece. Hope you can understand how unconditional love and affection can change an ordinary person into a marvellous one. Others can judge, have opinions, analyze your attitude, show you the real world; however the loved ones should be there to keep you in their magical world,

to heal you with their love potions.
Trust me, it works.

CHAPTER EIGHT

Twirl it!

One evening at my mom's place, my family members gathered in the living room. By that time my little girl started playing with the bangles by twirling it. She had just then learned how to play with the bangles. Out of rejoice, she started involving the other family members too in the game. One after the other; my grandfather, my mother, and finally I too joined the game. After a few minutes she felt bored as we were playing like this. She invited everyone to compete with her, except my grandmother.

I wanted her to learn the true spirit of the game. At the same time, we are not arrogant towards her. We will always help her to compete to our level of game. This keeps her encouraging every time to outshow her fullest potential.

Rewinding back to the evening, we had started a funny competition to see whose bangle would fall down first. Whenever someone wins the game, she rejoices by clapping her hands and insisting everyone of us to clap for her. Even she called my grandmother, who was busy watching a television serial, to join the little celebration. Initially, we felt like why the girl made everyone clap. As the game progressed, we forgot that we were adults and started rejoicing like my little girl whole heartedly. We felt lighter for a couple of hours.Though we made fun of her (not seriously) as an attention seeker, she was the one who made everyone active for at least 2 hours in the living room with the very simple game.

You may think, what's special about this? Can you recall an incident in the near future where you had rejoiced continuously without any call or a conversation like a child at least for an hour? If you miss to figure it out, I assure you that this episode will be a great life lesson.

Even I videographed the incident for the memory. Sometimes we might be busy in our work, ignoring the chottus calling us to play with them. As grown ups, we may feel that we will be bored within a few minutes of that simple game. I would suggest not to avoid that , it may turn into a great memory or it will teach us a life lesson.

• 16 •

CHAPTER NINE

A Complaint on Father

One evening when I returned home from work, my little girl received me with a complaint that her dad was not allowing her to wash the socks. She insisted that I reason with him.On being asked,he said that she has been playing in water for more than ten minutes and also wasting more water than required. I can understand the reason for his restriction, as she had a severe cold at that time.

I turned to my daughter, and I told her that her dad was correct. I instructed her to focus on other tasks. But she didn't leave it , ``Mom, You told me once that I am expected to take care of my things on my own, but why are you not allowing me to do so". Those words made me think a lot. I asked her to wait for a while. I changed and freshened up. I entered the bathroom to see how she was washing the socks. Since I didn't like to put the socks in the washing machine, I used to wash them myself. She had observed me and followed the same. But she forgot to soak. The stain was still there. She thought that by washing it off in running water , those stains will be washed away.

Though my husband was not interested in letting her work with water for a long time, I understood the concerns from both sides. I told my little girl that, observe carefully today how amma is washing the socks.Once you get well, you should implement the same to wash your socks. Both father and daughter agreed.

I made her sit outside the bathroom, and instructed how to soak and to remove the stains on the clothes with the brush.She was observing it carefully till I dried the socks. After two weeks, She showed me a pair of socks that were hung after washing. The socks were not fully cleaned. But they were better compared to the previous wash.I appreciated her for her work.A simple lesson had extended to her id card tag, kerchief and many other things she would wash.

It is important to notice that, addressing the problem or feeling concerned about their emotions are must. Apart from that, it is more important to teach how to rectify the shortcomes and how to do things properly.Once you inculcate these habits at an early age, they will never forget.

There is a phrase in Tamizh(Tamil) "pasumarathu aani pola", it means that, when you put a nail on a young tree, it will go inside smoothly and it will stay firm. If you do the same to an old tree, it would be comparatively hard. So, whatever you teach or guide them in their early age, it will enter into their mind easily and will be saved in their memory for a long time.It is in our control to select the things which would stay in their minds

CHAPTER TEN

Distractions are Helpful

Every mother is a soldier. They are always ready to face unreasonable anger, cry, joy, adamant nature etc. The only thing we are afraid to handle is their unreasonable tantrums. These tantrums may arise from improper sleep, lack of care from their loved ones, unaddressed complaints or statements etc. In simple words, when they feel their inability to handle a situation or a dialogue, they will start throwing tantrums at their opponents.

During this time, it is necessary to pacify them before they turn adamant or arrogant. Early address of any problem will reduce any unwanted dramas and dialogues.

There were umpteen number of situations where my little girl was throwing her tantrums.Some of them will be addressed at the very beginning, in turn it helps me in maintaining peace at home. When I could not figure out the reason for her tantrums,the pacifying dialogues would go in vain.Sometimes it would worsen the situation too.

At the same time, it is not possible to pacify her all the time.Even as a mother, I can't help her. Either it is a kid or an adult,self help is the best. She is too young to understand this.I started observing her activities, in which she was able to sit quietly for a long time. At this age,her solution lies in art and craft. Whenever I feel she is in high mood swings, I started to deviate her with art and craft for a while. Though it is not the perfect solution for all the situations, it helps her to restore her peace and in turn her thinking ability too. This helps her to make wise decisions and to avoid such mood swing or crankiness.

You might think that deviation will bring her distraction and her focus towards playing or main work may get affected. The truth is even if I am not distracting her, She can't concentrate on a single activity for more than half an hour. In fact that is quite common for all the children. At least by deviating her , I am guiding her to do something effectively rather than creating a mess.

CHAPTER ELEVEN

Consistency, Consistency,Consistency

"We are not in the right way of action, as we are thinking.Yet we are expecting the result of our thought process. When the result is for our action, we hesitate to accept it."

I always wanted to incorporate a reading habit in my daughter. I used to insist her to read any book other than academics for at least half an hour a day. As I strongly feel that books will open a new world to children.

One night,my little girl came to me and requested me to narrate a story for her. I was sleepy.I promised her a story the following night, to which she agreed and slept.The following night when she was bringing the book to me, I told her that I was tired that day too. The same continued for a couple of days. Then she left the concept of reading books and started engaging herself with her toys or games. Even I forgot things and kept myself busy with other work.

As months passed by quickly , one day I scolded her for playing with her toys and not being ready to learn stories, as I was free by that time.After the conversation,she accompanied me to hear the stories. That week I narrated her many fantasy stories.To attract children it's better to start with fantasy stories. Again the next week I was stuck with my work, so I was not able to narrate more stories during the bed time.

She pestered me to narrate the stories for one or two days and then she left. She was too young to read a book.Slowly her interest towards reading a book vanished. One day as an alarm in my mind, I started realizing the reading habit of my girl, then I promised myself to incorporate the habit again in her with consistency in priority list. Then, I could not fix it just for bedtime, but whenever I was free,I would induce her to take her story books to me to narrate the story or solve puzzles or to explain science or instill general knowledge.

Trust me it works! They learn it or not,the actions insisted and implemented by us daily will influence them to do their work regularly with consistency.Compared to me, my husband narrates a story to her daily during bedtime even if he is unwell.Just remember consistency and perseverance are two fertilizers, that helps the plant to grow well.

CHAPTER TWELVE

Exploring within the Limits

A few months back, we attended my sister's wedding. The marriage hall was quite big. Apart from the hall, the dining area, the parking lot, and the guest room area made the convention hall a majestic one. When it comes to weddings, comfort is usually replaced by adjustments. Being vast in its area itself became a disadvantage in managing my little one.

In Bangalore, she used to be in a small apartment with little floor space to play, she was so fascinated by the larger area, which made her fly like a butterfly here and there. Making her sit in a place itself is a big task. As that was my sister's wedding, I had to stand in the reception, and communicate with the people. Also, I was spending time with them. Meanwhile, she found a companion of her age, she would run to play with them. Keeping a track of her whereabouts and attending to guests at the same time became a hectic task.

Around 8 o'clock during the reception, I could not find her again. When I asked one after the other people there, most of them pointed in different directions. I was unable to find her even after a search of half an hour or so. The entire situation was scary for me. I almost felt a sinking feeling in my stomach, but I didn't want to worry everyone around.

My eyes were still scanning the hall, though I was talking to someone randomly. At one point, I found her at a distance along with some other kids, playing in the buffet area. As I don't want to miss her from my sight again, I ran towards her and held her. She was smiling at me and told me that she was playing with her little brothers. I don't know how to express that she should be safe, as we were aware of dangers around the society and she was too naive to understand that. Though I wanted to say many things, I just controlled myself and said, "You can play but don't be away from my eyesight."

However, she interpreted my message in her own way and said she was around familiar people in the hall. If she didn't know anyone in particular, she moved to the place where she knew someone.This gave me a big relief. I felt I should test the kid as to whether what she said is correct or not. But she was actually true to her words.

This taught me a big lesson to step out of my overprotective zone. This is the result of living in a nuclear family and residing in a place, where we don't know many people.We need to prepare them in an appropriate way to handle difficult situations. Our fear of the world and its negativity should not prevent them from exposure, which might not let them have their experiences and memories.

At Sister-in-law's Place

On a weekend morning, we visited my sister- in law's house. My little girl and her little boy started playing together. Till afternoon, both were fighting and often threw the words as they didn't want to play with each other.I was quite disgusted as I can't bear such dramas and I decided to take her back home. To my surprise, she refused to come with me and she insisted on playing with him.There is no wonder in that statement. Kids' moods will swing often.

My curiosity leads me to analyze now, what gives her comfort with him, which she could not feel a few hours ago.This is not the first time to get such a reply. Every time, when I try to come up with a reason for their behavior, they prove that it will be a wrong guess. When I strongly observe her pattern, I can understand that, if she is determined to face any kind of situation, she will be able to handle even the harder situations by herself. On the other hand, if she is forced by someone to adjust or face the situation, her crankiness will deactivate her frontal lobes that leads to her inability to handle it and in turn, it results in a teary situation or finding fault with others.

Now it is in our hands to develop their self responsibility, which is a very important quality for a child to increase their smartness and critical thinking in problem solving situations. It does not mean that all the 24 hours we should give such practical situations to deal with their problems. Instead, either it is a school or a home, wherever they could face a problem, that must be their learning centers. They can solve the problem or admit their mistakes to their peers or handle the situations smartly for the moment or sacrifice their feelings for better situations.

Whatever it is, they should learn to do it on their own. Only thing we can do as a parent is, Just observe how they are handling, guide them in a proper way when they are throwing tantrums to handle it wisely. At the moment, you are the coach,neither player nor a referee.Make your disciple to handle the situation through your guidance and prepare them for the unexpected twists and turns in their life,which should be a life lesson for them

CHAPTER FOURTEEN

Two Little Coins

One fine evening, I had taken her for shopping.She was fascinated by the things over there.Whatever she saw, she requested me to buy for her.I was giving various reasons for different things to why I was not buying the particular thing at the moment.She was frustrated at one point, ant started showing mild tantrums initially.Though I don't want to neglect that, I had no time left behind to address her tantrums. I pretended that I was not listening to her. Her tantrums and adamancy started growing, which I could feel in her actions or words. It was about to rain and I had to take her back home in a two - wheeler.

I rushed to the cash counter, paid the bill and about to step out of the shopping store. She started refusing to come with me without purchasing a toy, which we had already at home in a mini version.I tried to explain to her that we would not require the toy,but she was not in a mood to listen to me.

Then I picked up a colorful toy, which she didn't have, and offered that toy, only if she was ready to give up the toy that she wanted. Initially she was reluctant, later she was ready to go with my offer.We reached home at perfect timing, as it started raining cats and dogs, the moment we stepped in.

She started playing with her new toy.I too got indulged with my work, but something was running in my mind that I should uproot her behavior within the next shopping trip. After signing off from all of my work, I went to bed. She too joined me and pestered me to tell a story.Initially I had an idea to inculcate this moral through a story, but I could figure out the non - progressive outcomes for that.

Then suddenly I handed over a ten rupee note to her and told, next time whatever she wanted to buy, she could buy from her savings. I discussed the same with my husband. So we had decided to give her ten rupees every Friday.It was up to her to buy an expensive toy by saving the amount or a cheap one for that moment.Even that ten rupees would make a difference in her behaviour.As we explained the things, she was also happy.

In course of time, She started saving the money and stopped herself from buying unwanted stuff.As she watches us for spending on others, she too will be saying that she will buy gifts for her cousins from the money she had saved. We were glad to see her healthy attitude.

We went to our hometown one day, immediately after getting down from the car, she rushed to her grandparents and handed over a few coins to them and told in her innocent voice that she could not buy anything for them, so she requested to accept the coins and with that they could buy whatever they needed. Though the amount was very less, they happily accepted the money from her with pride and tears as one little heart was there to show concern to them. Her gestures made the moment a loving memory.

A small idea shaped her into an empathetic human, What else does a parent need from their kids? Thanks to the universe!

CHAPTER FIFTEEN

A Little Brain is under Construction

In course of time, It is quite common with the parents and the teachers to treat the children as an adult.On seeing the children daily and conversing with them, we eventually forget that their brain is still developing.

We conveniently expect that, if we ask them to be quiet, they should be quiet. If we ask them to be patient, they should be patient.We may think that they know the meaning of all words, what we utter and they are capable of understanding all the situations. Instead, we must take a breath, they are still chottus.We all know that the brain development will take place until the age of 25.But we are rushing a 4 year or 10 year old kid to understand all the things. Teaching the values or incorporating the values are different from our full pledged expectations.

For example: As both the parents are working nowadays, they hardly manage the time to spend with their kids on a daily basis.When the quality time is not spent, it is foolish to expect that the children will obey their parents.The parents bribe the children to get the work done.In turn,the child learns to become greedy and selfish.The children obey their parents' words for that particular time, if they feel the offer is worth it. Or else they demand for another offer or deny to do the task given to them.

When they obey, the parents take that as a moment of great achievement. Unknowingly they develop the corporate ideologies, not the moral values in that young mind, which doesn't have a word called empathy in it. If a child is ready to help a parent or a friend or a neighbour, it should be out of empathy and not for an offer.

How can we incorporate moral values in children? There are two ways, either through the real life incident or moral stories.Not all the children are mature enough to extract the moral values from the real life situations.It's always better to go with the moral fantasy stories.Repeat the stories often . Slowly and steadily you can feel the change in your young ones.

CHAPTER SIXTEEN

Struggles are the Pebbles

As generations pass, few things remain as fresh as its origin. One among them is giving our best to our heirs. Until the previous generation, it was the sons who enjoyed the comfort, now the daughters too joined the list. According to eastern people's mindset, we should struggle utmost to provide the best to our sons or daughters, right from education to life.

Earlier people strived to give the best education,which was welcomed. Later started spending so much of time and money in marriages to provide the best part of the remaining life. Though they convince us by saying that our kids should not be abused both economically and physically after marriage which leaves some imprints on the hard work by our children.

Nowadays, parenting has reached its worst stage, as both the parents are working.They compromise their time with their kids with the toys or games or pocket money, which in turn makes them step into the new lazy and super comfort zone. Apart from the kids' needs, we are ready to provide our childhood desires, replicas of neighborhood toys as we didn't teach and want our kids to share their toys.

As a gem of the crown, we are not sharing our struggles to our kids, which in turn sometimes kids treat us as a money vending machine instead of learning empathy towards parents.Here is the short story, how I am sharing my feelings and other things with her.

From the time I conceived, I started sharing all my feelings right from happiness to depression in a proper proportion to my fetus.After 8 months of pregnancy, I could feel the reaction of my feotus according to my moods and words. Though I had more complications in giving a normal birth, she might have heard my words so as not to discomfort me a lot, as a feotus she helped me in delivering her by normal birth.

Right from her birth, I express my feelings to her. If I struggle for her, I will convey that. If I feel happy for her, I will say that. Same with anger and other feelings too. At one point, she started developing empathy towards me.She started reading my feelings to some extent.If I am not happy with her activities, She will say sorry, and do something that makes me happy. She started caring for me like an adult.

Sometimes I could feel that I am reaping for what I had sown in her. Though many times people scolded me for sharing my anger or depression to my kid, I know in what proportion I am sharing it. At the same time she should understand how her parents are managing things for her.

Always, don't forget that the charity begins at home.

CHAPTER SEVENTEEN

A Very Rare Combination

Usually we are not the parents who fight in front of our little girl.Compared to me my husband is very cautious in that.But one night, a small spark between us turned into a big fight. Although it is common for couples to fight and reunite, it will not be that easy for our little one to overcome such things. We could not even imagine how their minds would interpret our emotions, words, reactions while we are fighting. We would be back to normal after a few hours but they would not come out of it that easily.

That day, I don't know how I lost my mind.As the fight got intense, my husband walked out of the home stating that he had to purchase a few items. Even though I felt that I needed a break by that time, I didn't stop him. Meanwhile, my daughter was observing all the things happening around us.

I was feeling upset about the fight that happened.She came near me and told," Amma, don't cry and feel for dad's words. Sometimes he will scold me too for not doing my work, But I will not feel or cry. Instead I will say to myself that I will not feel bad for his scoldings. I will leave the things to happen on its way. I will keep myself happy. You too try to keep yourself happy"

I could not even imagine that these words are from a four year old girl. I am completely astonished by her approach towards others' scoldings and happenings in life. Really gifted maturity. I always like her innocence blended with the right proportion of maturity, which is a very rare combination.This time I left speechless as it showered some enlightenment on me.Though I used to say happiness lies in us, in some situations we forget to remember our own words. This universe is very powerful to give back to us in the right time, whatever we give it to others as words or actions.

It would take at least a day for me to be normal after such a fight. But with her words, I went back to normal within a few hours.But it was late night to talk to my husband. The next morning I talked to my husband. I felt sorry for the fight. Though I was strong in my view, I expressed it in a better way rather than in anger. He too realized his mistakes and put forward his points. By the time the fight came to an end, my little girl also jumped out of bed and shared our hugs and kisses. The happiness in her face was like, she deserved that.I thanked the universe for the wonderful family and started my routine.

CHAPTER EIGHTEEN

A Devil

"Anger blocks our thoughts and makes us blind." Whenever we get angry we forget about our circumstances places, people, surroundings etc. We are ready to vent out the anger as the instances grow like a balloon. Even when the unknown person is ready to prick us too, we will burst in full force.

Sometimes the anger balloon which got bursted in front of the adults (known or unknown) could not be an acceptable one. The opponent who observed your anger might not come out of the situation for a while. Just imagine if your kid is exposed to your anger burst. How cruel and pathetic it would be! It will take a few months or even years to recover from the incident.

It is not necessary that they should be the victim of your anger. They may also be spectators. The feelings are always intense with children ranging from fear to embarrassment. Though it was late, I realized this at one point of my life.

There was a meaningless fight between me and my husband. Since I had not recovered completely from postpartum depression, even a single word can elate my anger at times. Though I regained my control over my thoughts and actions, sometimes it would be an immense failure. That day too a single word from my husband drove me crazy and when the anger reached its peak, I had started throwing tantrums both in words and actions, at one point I told him that I will jump from the balcony.

My mind entirely forgot to notice that my little one was watching my agony with tears. I was not in a state to analyze my words and actions. After that incident everything was back to normal in a few days. My little one went to native the following week, where she addressed her concern in front of everyone that her mom (that was me) told that she would jump from the balcony after a fight with her dad. My mom didn't make it an issue nor asked me about this as she knew, the fight between husband and wife never lasts long and she was aware of both of our attitudes and love towards each other. She had ended the scenario to my daughter in a very comic way as my little one never remembered that.

This incident was narrated by my husband as he made me understand the seriousness of the issue that happened that day. On learning about that, I felt bad and realized how my actions and words affected my kid. Though many times I had promised myself not to manipulate my anger, I failed at times. But this was an eye-opening incident for me. Since then I have tried to control my anger, deviating it when it gets manipulated. Also I have tried to be very vigilant with my words. Keep calm (both inside and outside), the world is beautiful.

CHAPTER NINETEEN

Is Staying Apart a Gift?

Either it is a working mother or a housewife, all we need is a break. Break means it should be a proper break. At least two days in a month, we need a rest from our routine work, both at home and career. If I mention home it should be a day off from serving kids, husband and other family members. We should sleep whenever we feel like, eat whatever we like, go for a ride or walk if we prefer to, hang out with our friends or neighbours for a while etc. In our society, rest for a woman is considered only a day off from her job or having dinner with a family in a month.

If a woman has a toddler, her break lies if someone takes care of her baby for a while. If a woman has many family members at home, for her break means to be on a long ride or going outstation with her husband. So, at one point she feels that she should be left alone even without her kids. Many will not confess this openly because of the society, which here revolves around the baby. Many questions will be attacking her, saying that there is no enjoyment without the baby. Of course, I agree, but once in a while we too need a complete break.

I am lucky to have my husband by my side as he is understandable in such things. He respects my privacy, indeed he is the person who advises me to meet my friends as I don't much prefer to go out without my family. When I started to go out with my friends, once in a while, I could understand my full rejuvenation as I felt more comfortable with friends. I should thank him for this.

When I started to go out, apart from my husband I had to think of my little girl too. Either it is an hour or a day out, I am concerned about her. I don't want to lie to her about it . Initially she was a little bit reluctant, but she started understanding me as she understood the importance of the friends during her play time etc. Now either it is my day out or hers (like visiting native or day out to a relatives place or simply with her dad) she happily sends off me or biding bye and accepts my absence.This maturity she attained because of my husband's advice.

The moment you feel that your feelings are considered, you feel blessed as I am now. Touch wood...... Thanks to the Universe!!

CHAPTER TWENTY

Be Firm with Decisions

Most of the time, I will not get my daughter ready for school, as I go to work early. It's my husband who wakes her up and sends her to school. One day when it was a holiday for me but not for her, I took charge, everything went smooth, until I started organizing her snacks, water bottle and lunch in her lunch bag. The moment I touched her lunch bag, she screamed and told me not to pack the things in the lunch bag, instead to keep it in her school bag itself.

I replied that the curry would be leaked, your books would be spoiled. But she didn't want to listen at all. She was very determined in not carrying the lunch bag. Initially I thought it might be an additional burden to a little girl to carry both the bags. I left the issue there and started packing the things as she had very few books to carry.

Another day, a similar situation happened. But this time I was determined to give lunch bag as her school bag is already heavy. She was so firm not to take a lunch bag, this made me smell some other reasons behind this. While dressing her up, I genuinely asked her what was the reason for not carrying the lunch bag. She replied that her ma'am insisted her not to bring two bags. For instance, I trusted her words and suddenly I recalled a few parents sending lunch bags with them. This time in a strict tone, I asked her to confess the truth. I told her that I will clarify with her ma'am.

This time with a slight fear, she told me I don't like that lunch bag style, as she needed it in pink. Though I was angry, I didn't want to show it to her. Politely I asked, who accompanied me, while buying lunch bags? She replied that it was her. Then I asked who selected brown instead of pink that day, she agreed that it was herself. But she argued that she didn't like it now.

I made her sit on my lap and explained to her with real life incidents of other children that we should not step back from our choices, though everyone will say, it is her wish, at that point you will start losing your respect, if you step back of your own choice. Next time the trust on your choice or selection will be reduced to others.

It is wise to take time to make a decision but once you have decided, you should adhere to it. If you are confused about how to select something, you can take help from some wise persons. At the same time, if you don't like something, you have full rights to oppose that. You don't want to be afraid of anyone. Be bold with your voices.

As my stories and advice slowly got infused in her, she came out with a bold statement that," I don't like what I have selected this time, but next year I need a pink lunch bag." My mission was a success, also I nodded my head for her obligation as it contained truth, boldness and understanding.

CHAPTER TWENTY-ONE

An Admiration Helps

A child's first admiration is the mother. No matter how the mother is, they will laugh, smile or admire you right from birth. But this admiration will start reducing to some extent. as the child starts observing the other humans. They just move towards their supporters. A mother cannot always be a supporter of what the children do. We should be strict at many times to shape the child.

Also if the admiration is getting reduced, the mother will start losing her control over her kids. If a kid listens to a mom, they should admire her first. Admiration doesn't come off only with the external beauty, but also with the knowledge and respect that we earn.

It's not only the teacher or the school to be updated one to give the best to our kids, we should also be equally updated with our knowledge in various fields especially the area where the kids' interest lies.Though sometimes we feel its unnecessary, the child will accept your words, only when they feel you as a mentor, guide,peer and well wisher. Apart from being a parent, we have to play these many roles.

My little one will obey my words even today. I am a strict mom, whenever it is required. She accepts my strictness too. You may think, how is it possible? Here speaks the update in parenting method and also I have improved myself in her area of interests such as art and craft, dance etc., to spend some non-academic quality time together.

This makes her feel that I am there for her to share her feelings. And for kids, either they throw tantrums or express their real feelings, all we need is to listen first and to the fullest. Then we should analyze and give proper guidance. Even after they throw tantrums, we should be strict in expressing our feelings towards their attitude and if you feel like punishing them, it should be a mold or a productive one.

Always remember that punishment or negligence should not hurt them, instead it should give some space to realize their mistakes and get back on the right track. Every child is unique. You can find a way to manage your child through trial and error. But while trying the methods , just keep the above said points in mind.

CHAPTER TWENTY-TWO

Shower the Gratitude

As I have some health issues, I often fall sick which even I don't like. Every time it's my husband and my daughter who takes care of me. In some circumstances my blood pressure went low, and I was not in condition to go for work nor do any household work. Meanwhile, my daughter's first term examination had also arrived. Unfortunately, my husband had to report back to work from the same week.

I was left to take care of myself. I could do nothing. That night, I was helping my little one in her exam preparations. After her preparations she was lying on my lap and trying to convey that she was not ready to go to school.Though I don't want to encourage that, I was a little bit curious to know what is the reason behind her statements. I started digging deep into the statements with the conversation.

Me: Don't you want to go to school?

She: No.

Me: Why?

She: Simply.

Me: Don't you want to write your examinations?

She: I do.

Me: Then what is the problem?

She: I feel like not going to school now, as dad is also going to the office.

Me: Staring at her, I told her if you are not letting me know the real reason, I will not be listening to your talks anymore.

She: (paused for a while). Maa, if dad is going to the office and if I also go to school, who is there to take care of you?

The moment she uttered these words, I could feel my heart racing, for my sake, she refused to go to school.Also I had a strong feeling that she is my second mom who is caring and understanding.That moment I have concluded that my little one deserves this book.

Then I made her understand that I was okay and manageable at home alone and she can take care of me after school hours. She agreed to some extent and went to sleep.I kissed her on her forehead with a sight full of love and gratitude. Though we say everything is a reflection/reaction of what we give, I feel it is what they observe and learn too.The way she consumes the positive thoughts and actions from her surroundings along with her innocence which always leaves me in wonderment.

In today's world everyone is running behind money or fame, literally even the person who cares or loves us the most.They don't have time to inquire about our health. It's quite common in this era. But my humble request is to respect those people who inquire about your health at least once when you are not well and be grateful to the person who takes care of you in spite of all their busy schedules.Just thank the universe for being surrounded with such people in your life.

CHAPTER TWENTY-THREE

No Fun with Fashion

Dressing is the only way that you communicate your personality or mood to others without actually communicating. In Fact it is an effective non-verbal communication. I am not here to talk about the freedom of wearing dresses, But how much are we trained to select a dress that fits our body, skin tone etc.?

The most comfortable dress gives us more confidence in the public arena. We have to be very cautious with our attire. The most confident people don't spend unnecessary time being cautious on their attire, their focus will be on efficiency and they manage their time efficiently. You can have a self check on various occasions where you wore uncomfortable dresses. We feel it should be the most taught subject to our child. It all started with my husband.

My husband is very cautious about our dresses outside our home. All he demands is that our dress should be neat, decent and comfortable. There are no restrictions to any wears. Even if it is a western wear, it should fit the above criteria.We will not interfere in each other's dressing sense. If we want our dress to be a matching outfit, I will request him to wear it in the shades on which we dressed up.

As fashion evolves, it is completely useless to talk about old age traditional dresses. We wear comfortable outfits both at home and at the workplace. If someone compels us which dress we should wear on a particular day or on a daily basis, it is no wonder that we will feel angry at the person. If that is the scenario, it is no wonder that our kids feel angry with us too, when we restrict them in the modern era. Also if we feel that our kid should dress sensibly when they are nearing their teenage years. We should be sensible enough to guide them about their dressing sense since their childhood. They should not feel contradictory in our words or thoughts.

As parents we have been very clear about this since my little one's childhood. At the same time we are not the one to pick the dresses for her. When she turned four, we gave space to select the dresses on her own. Initially she struggled to pick the comfortable ones, now she is somewhat trained herself even to select the best colour combinations and the accessories that suit her dress along with the comfortable and decent dresses for her. Anywhere we had not restricted the category ethnic or western etc.,but we guided her after trying on a dress, which suits her. We even ask her to sit, walk and roam for 2 -3 min to make her understand the comfort of the dress she chose.

Always the advice or theory will not work to the core, only the practice makes a man perfect.

CHAPTER TWENTY-FOUR

A Rush will not Push

One fine evening, when we were returning from one of our relative's houses, I asked my husband to stop near a grocery shop to buy a few items for the next day. Suddenly my little girl told me that she needed chocolate to present to her friend on her birthday.

I replied that she will give you chocolate on her birthday, so you need not buy a chocolate for her. Then her tone had a coat of adamancy that she needed chocolate. Fine, I started buying groceries with the explanation to her. I refused her because she had a bad cold and cough. Even though I bought it for her friend she could not resist herself from eating chocolates which will make her cold even worse.

Even after explaining this, she was so adamant to buy a chocolate for herself. Then as usual I had started digging the reason for her stubbornness. After a few questions she replied that in her class for birthday kids, the other students are giving chocolates.Then the issue should be handled in a different manner. I then completed the shopping fast and returned home.

After dinner, we went to bed, where I found my little one was still upset. I slowly started talking to her. She was not ready to listen to my explanation as sometimes peer pressure is too strong irrespective of age than parental advice. I talked about healthy and unhealthy foods taught by her teacher the previous week. She started responding and slowly explained to her in a playful manner that we should follow what she learns, and quoted the application part as the place where real education starts its journey in everyone.

She was confused then. I explained the importance of application, cheat day to have fun, having control over decisions and our determinations through various stories and her life incidents from childhood to connect her well with the concepts. Finally I made her agree to give me something that should be hand made by her.

Either it is food or an art, if we do it for others for an occasion, that will be a special gift always irrespective of size or cost. The next morning she made a beautiful greeting card, though it was not like the one in a shop , her time and interest for the card is the love she showers on her friend. I appreciated her efforts. She happily gifted the same to her friend.

Don't rush into things while handling peer pressure, as it has a strong influence on the young minds, even adults too, from buying a shirt/ saree to a house /car. It will take its own time depending on the situation to put them back on track. Give space and allow them to come back on their own.

CHAPTER TWENTY-FIVE

Sparkling Smartness

Kids are always smart. No kids are exempt from that. After a day of hectic work, I went to bed by 9:00 p.m. But my husband and my little one were already there in the room playing with a ball by striking it against the wall. When I entered the room, they kept quiet for a while and looked at each other with a puzzle in their sight.

Yes, you guessed it right. I want to sleep, so I will not allow such disturbances inside the bedroom during our bed time. But they were in a very good mood to play. I told my husband strictly that I will hide the ball once it comes to me.

My daughter ignored my concern and started playing the ball. To her surprise it gave a nice blow to my right ear. You people could imagine my thought process at that time. Yes I was in anger, but as that was the first time, I was quite clear not to affect their enthusiasm. I just gave the second and strict warning that they should not play inside. I asked my husband whether she had a nap in the afternoon. He replied that she slept almost for three hours. It was obvious that she would not sleep until the clock struck twelve o' clock.

Then I explained to my girl politely that I need to sleep well to get rid of my body ache and to revitalize myself for the next day. Initially she was pleasing or requesting me to sleep in the living space. I was not ready for that. Suddenly she started massaging my legs, I gave a puzzled look at her. She told me that she would massage my legs, and told me to sleep well. She massaged my legs, back, hands and head. Though the pressure was not enough to enjoy the pleasure of the massage, her efforts made me feel it. Then slowly she said that she wanted to play ball inside, so she requested me to lie down in the living room for a while.

Then I considered her request. Also explained to her that it will disturb my sleep as I will be switching rooms. Without expecting her reply, I went outside to sleep since she should not get the feeling that her polite request would be denied. I personally thought that would set a wrong example. They started playing again.

The next night, she was requesting her father to play ball before my bedtime. When I entered the room, she kept the ball aside and demanded a story to tell her. On hearing a few stories she slept off. The parents should be very clear that the children's attitude towards you is just the reflection of your attitude towards them. Always teach the values through your actions or deeds.

At the same time express your appropriate feelings to your kids. Don't think they are too young. At the same time, don't expect absolute understanding from them. They are learning. They will get shaped by themselves with our approach.

CHAPTER TWENTY-SIX

My Plate of Tensions

We are not interested in leaving our kid in daycare. The metro life demands earnings from couples. More than a caretaker, we feel her school premises are safer and more comfortable. She would also have friends to play with at daycare than have solitude at home with a caretaker.

The first day is very hectic for me, as I have to pack a lunch and two different snacks and other things mentioned by her caretaker at school.

Once I got everything ready, I went to my workplace. That day I was extremely disturbed as I could not take care of her. Also that she was not willing to go to daycare was making me feel low. Immediately I left the workplace once the clock struck 4 o'clock in the evening. It will take me a maximum of 45 minutes to reach her place. I am a slow rider in general, that day I didn't know how fast I had ridden my scooter, and I reached the destination within 30 minutes, in spite of the traffic.

In the rush, I forgot that the school would have a doorbell to ring. I tried calling her teacher, but she had not picked up the call. I was unable to control my anger and other emotions as the school door was also closed, and I could not enter inside to fetch my girl. At that moment, all I wanted was to see her. I called my husband and narrated the scenario, and he reminded me of the doorbell. At the same time, her caretaker called me back saying that she would bring my little one to me in the next 5 minutes.

I was going through a turmoil of emotions. When I saw her near the gate, a few tears were already kissing my cheeks. To my utter shock, she was also not happy with my arrival. I hope the readers can understand my helplessness. I tried to control my emotions at that time. I picked her up and left for home.

While riding the scooter, She was sitting behind me. I asked her about the first day at her daycare. She said that she was okay in a low voice. If she was okay with the daycare, I was puzzled by the dullness on her face.

Thinking that she might not have had a good sleep in the afternoon, as her caretaker also told me that she didn't sleep,so she was drawing all the time.

After reaching home, I insisted that she could sleep for some time. However, she told me that she was angry with me, which made my feelings even worse. I made her sit on my lap and gave a detailed explanation of our option to put her in daycare. Suddenly, she jumped out of my lap and told me that she was not angry about leaving her in daycare, as she enjoyed the time with her friends there. That was so puzzling. I didn't interrupt her, she went on to say why did I come to pick her up so early? I was perplexed. I asked her what she meant. She told me that she wanted to eat snacks with her friends in the evening and also wanted to play some more, but I picked her up early. I burst out laughing for a moment and I agreed to pick her up by 5:30 in the evening.

I was just thinking about her longing for people and how my brain fooled me when I was emotionally arrested by a situation. The harder situations always make me wise either financially or emotionally.

CHAPTER TWENTY-SEVEN

My Mom's Birthday

It's very common to forget our own birthdays when we are aging. The reason may be due to work pressure or health conditions causing us to run behind the money or career. Though we argue that relationships and people are more important than money, in the practical world, we need money even to satisfy those relationships.

When it is very hard to remember our own birthday. It is even harder to remember other people's birthdays. Even if we remember each other's birthday also, we will remember it on that particular day. We are unable to buy chocolates for them. Though we remember and wish our near and dear ones on their birthday, we fail to update other people to wish them which would give them immense joy. The usual reason we give is that we forgot due to our busy work schedule. Though it sounds dramatic, it is the ground reality too.

Such an incident happened in my life. In the early morning, when I was about to start the day, I tore a daily calendar sheet.When I saw the date, suddenly my memory rings an alarm that it is my mom's birthday. I was about to call, my daughter woke up from the bed and told me she too would join the call.Then we freshened up and called her, we wished her. She was surprised by our wish as she had forgotten her own birthday. Then I talked to her for a few minutes and returned to my work.

While I was preparing breakfast, I heard my daughter speaking to someone on video call. I was over hearing her words to know whom she was speaking to. She called my sister but her son was attending the call. He is younger than my daughter. She shared that, that day was their grandmother's birthday, she wished her and insisted that he should surprise my mom by wishing her. That little human also replied that he would wish her. They were talking about the gift plans(simply their hand made scribbled cards, presenting toys from their toy bags etc.,).Finally she asked him to inform my sister too.That was a very sweet conversation that lasted for more than 10 minutes.

Then they did a group video call, which I could not attend because of my work. I was thinking no one would insist her to inform my sister about my mom's birthday, yet this little girl felt happy to spread happiness to my mom through their wishes too. As I was also not near to buy even a sweet for her, I could remind her birthday to her near and dear ones, which would have made her birthday even more special.

We should accept that, sometimes our younger versions are reminding us of our forgotten days.

CHAPTER TWENTY-EIGHT

My Little Girl's Warmth

Nowadays, we have no option other than leaving her in daycare.We have been preparing her for a long time now, that she would be going to daycare. She constantly resisted the idea. .Sometimes she even asked me to leave my job to take care of her.

One day, she was talking to my mother-in-law over the phone. She was asking about her interests in the day care. I was very eager to know what answer she would say, as all the grandparents are against daycare. She stared at me for a while which gave me an idea that today I will be advised on quitting my career.

But to my surprise, she started explaining the facilities in the daycare such as: play area, indulging time in art and craft with the other children, spending some quality time with the teacher etc. She almost repeated all the reasons we gave her. Also finally added a word which made me quite emotional and proud at the same time.

She told them that she has no other choice other than accepting the daycare.This answer was purely a reflection of her mind which made both the ends to feel for her unwillingness. At that moment my in-law asked her to request me to be at home and take care of her. To which she replied that she could manage in daycare as mom also should take care of her career. She respects my career and quest for my identity.This gave me a feeling of understanding towards her.

She is not an extraordinary kid, she is a very normal kid with usual adamancy, tantrums, childishness,love for her parents etc. Many times, she has irritated me with her rigidity but she will wipe out all those vibes with her understanding nature.

Not only with our parents, in umpteen situations she didn't let us down with anyone.This may be her inborn character or she incorporated the values through our teachings. But this is one of the finest values she ever learnt, which will take her to heights in the future.

All my principles are here to make her understand the values and make sure she inculcates the same in future. This is what I feel is the real and practical parenting.

CHAPTER TWENTY-NINE

Organize it!

Most kids will desire something, they will be adamant about getting that particular object. The undesirable part of this drama is as soon as they get whatever they want, they will not respect that. Their interest in that particular object vanishes suddenly. Many may argue that you would have bought them immediately. You should have delayed, made them understand the value of the object, and then you should have purchased it. All the theories don't work practically.

My little girl was constantly requesting me to buy her a watch for more than 4 months. I was delaying that for various reasons as she doesn't know how to read even the digital clock timings, moreover, watches are not allowed in her school, etc. Then I taught her how to read the time on a clock, then on a watch, and advised her not to show off with her friends, etc. In those four months, she learnt the same and she nodded for all my conditions.

Finally, I ordered a watch for her with light effects, which she loved the most. She was with the watch for the whole first day. The very next morning I found it lying down somewhere without proper care. This made me angry, as we are working hard even to earn a single rupee. This is the same watch wanted for several months.I felt to teach a lesson.

I left the watch as it was. I kept on observing whether she would organize it in the proper place. But she was busy with other toys. Later, I pretended to sweep the house, but by that time she had no idea about the watch. I just swept the watch in front of her and was about to put it in the dustbin. On seeing this, she came to me and requested me to return her watch. Then I reminded her about her demand and my investment in that. Also warned her, if it is not kept in the proper place, it would be thrown in the dustbin without a second thought. She understood to some extent.

In course of time, She understood that I would do the same thing with any of her toys or things if she didn't take care. I can't say she is a very well-organized girl at present, but I have definitely sowed the seed. I can witness the improvement in her, as she was taking care of her things.

One thing I understood well about the current generation of kids is that guiding or advising them should be a constant and continuous process. Until we feel that they have incorporated the values in them. So many distractions are there in the form of influence from their friends, neighbors, and social media, etc., To do that we need patience and perseverance as we are supposed to answer their questions, tolerate their opposition, etc., We should be very determined in the final output and we should not get carried away by the midway distress in the guiding process.

Let us reap the desired fruit from our children.

CHAPTER THIRTY

A Respect for Food

Food is an essential part of life. Of course, everyone is earning to their capacity to have the basic things in their lives. Until we get something we long for that, once that is available easily, we are not respecting that. From our elders, we used to hear a story as they struggled even for a balanced nutritional meal. But with this generation, we have a wide variety of options in foods. The investment is up to you either on healthy foods or unhealthy foods.

It's our duty to incorporate the value of food into our children. My husband and I are maximum cautious about not wasting food. To be honest, before marriage I would not care about such things even after much advice from my mom, as there is my granny to support me. After marriage, the entire scenario changed, as I started cooking, I felt that my labor for the kitchen work was fulfilled with the emptying of dishes.

Apart from wasting the dishes, one more thing that irritates me is spilling the food, which I hate to the core. My daughter is the exact opposite of us. She used to waste food often. Spilling is a scenario in which she could not have control. We have tried many ways, like showing how difficult it is to produce rice through a video, which was a great failure, as she could not understand the pain behind the production.

Then I tried to narrate some moral stories like how Thiruvalluvar will not waste food and respect it. That also went in vain. Then I showed the children who are all hungry and suffering for even a single bowl of rice. That brought a slight change but didn't last for more than a month.

I understood one thing, this has to be felt from within, not through a process, stories, or examples. Next week, during her non-school hours I stopped asking whether she needed something to eat or drink. This was the first thing, I made her realize her hunger first, which most mothers including me failed to do. So that she will not waste the food during non-school hours, as she needs the food for her hunger.

Then I slowly shifted from open choices to closed choices, so that she should try all the things. Now her appetite is good. She knows when to eat and how much is enough for her in a day. She has control over her food.

But the spilling is not rectified. Though I was teaching her it's not a good habit, she is in no mood to listen. Then for a week, I cut down her entertainment while eating, as the distractions are low, and the spilling was reduced. Since we both are working, That too didn't last long. Then I made her clean, if she refused to clean, It would not be cleaned by anyone. No other option for her other than to clean her table. Although she is still spilling now, it has been reduced. She is more cautious these days.

It is very difficult to inculcate a habit in a kid, but once you do, they will follow it for their lifetime. The First 7 years of a kid are very important in inculcating moral values and habits in them, where the parents' role is 90%. We are the influencers of our kids. Though a child is prone to its surroundings, The learning from parents is still higher than that of surroundings.